Conversation with

JESUS

Cover & Graphic Design

Mattias Långström

Conversation with

JESUS

✳✳✳

Copyright © Jan Fahleman

Publisher: **BHAGWAN 2022**

PREFACE

Bible quotes are often used both by church priests but also by the general public. Some Bible quotes have become winged words and are used to illustrate or exemplify something in everyday life. Why are these ancient quotes from Jesus time on earth so interesting to use in today's language? Well, because they are timeless truths and spiritual gold nuggets that come from a timeless spiritual foundation. However, one can interpret what Jesus said in many different ways. Over the years, Christianity has split into many different churches and denominations and there are different interpretations of the Bible quotes. In principle, you can say that you either interpret them according to a certain tradition or you interpret them as you experience them. In the latter case, one can assume that there can be as many interpretations as there are people here on earth.

It can also be said that for one and the same person, for a certain Bible quote, there may be different interpretations depending on what level of spiritual awareness you are at when you make the interpretation. It can vary during different phases of life such as children, teenager, adult or during old age.

Should one therefore avoid making an interpretation? No, the interpretation is to anchor the Bible quotes in

*both the external relative existence, i.e. in the mind
and intellect but at the same time in the inner conscious existence that thirsts for spiritual knowledge. Every
human being should make himself independent of old
interpretations that depend on someone else's insights
from the past and allow his own interpretation that rests
on the basis of his own experiences from the past and in
the present.*

*To allow the "Kingdom of Heaven that is within you" to
have the opportunity to appear. To let the attention go
inward and listen without prejudice to the message that
then emerges. One cannot say that one's own interpretation is more true than someone else's interpretation,
but one can experience that a certain interpretation can
mean that one sees from a perspective where one is united with the Kingdom of Heaven, i.e. the level of spiritual consciousness, which can be described as the eternal
unlimited Consciousness of God, instead of letting the
limited mind and intellect emerge and dominate.
The state of consciousness "Kingdom of Heaven" can be
seen from three different perspectives; based on a belief
that you have a dualistic relationship with, i.e. me and
the Kingdom of Heaven or something that you have
experienced, i.e. something that you experience or have
experienced but still have a dualistic relationship with
or something that you are present in, i.e. has a non-dual
relationship to.*

To say that one has a non-dualistic relationship with God can be considered by some as blaspheming God. It is believed that the union with God could only take place by Jesus or saints and prophets in historical times and not today. Being spiritually rooted in the Kingdom of Heaven is considered to be something that was only bestowed on Jesus, the prophets and the wise men in biblical times. It is said that; in the present, only faith can bind man to God. But Jesus does not agree with this. In his statements and through advice to people, he shows the way to the Kingdom of Heaven in the present, no matter what age one lives in. The "Holy Spirit" is present in eternity and gives spiritual light, knowledge and wisdom to the one who is ready to receive it and become perfect and aware in Godconsciousness.

Jesus was aware in Godconsciousness. His statements come directly from the Consciousness of God as wisdom. This wisdom is not bound to a particular epoch but is rooted in eternity. For the word God, Jesus used various words or concepts such as; the Father, the Kingdom, the Kingdom of God, the Kingdom of Heaven, and the Helper; the Holy Spirit. I have in my comments even used; Consciousness or the Godconsciousness.

The following questions, with answers via biblical quotes from Jesus, can be seen as a fictitious meeting with Jesus that gives rise to a different interpretation of the biblical quotations than the interpretation given by traditional Christianity.

Jan Fahleman

Where is the Kingdom of Heaven?

1 . Jesus: The kingdom of God will not come through observation, and men will not say, see, it is here! Or, there! For the kingdom of God is within you. Luke 17: 20-21. What is central and fundamental in this statement is that "the Kingdom of Heaven is within you." Jesus says that the Kingdom of Heaven is within you and that the Kingdom of God is within you. It is already there, you do not have to hope or believe that it will come in the future. What matters is to make contact with it and be aware in it in the present.

The consciousness of God, the Kingdom of Heaven, is not a physical place but a state of consciousness. So it is not located so you can see it. It is eternal and "omnipresent" i.e. everywhere present. It is also omniscient, i.e. have knowledge that includes total existence.

When Jesus says that it exists within you, he does not mean that it exists somewhere inside the body. What he means is that attention must be shifted from the external to the internal existence. From the outer relative changing sensual existence to the inner spiritual eternal existence of the Soul, to the Kingdom of Heaven, the Holy Spirit i.e. Godconsciousness which is the kingdom of God.

Everything is Godconsciousness. To be present in the Consciousness of God is to be in the Kingdom of Heaven. To be constantly in the Kingdom of Heaven and at the same time be awake, asleep or dreaming is to be fully present and aware.

Since it is there within us, what is it then that prevents us from getting in touch with it? It is as if a fish swimming in water becomes thirsty and wonders how it will be able to drink water. The solution is that the fish only need to open its mouth to become unthirsty. In the same way it is when it comes to getting in touch with the Kingdom of Heaven. It does not have to be something complicated that requires years of theological study and sacred commitment or that one has lived a life totally without sin. Letting attention shift from the domains of the mind and ego to inner attention is what is required: to become aware of the external, changing, relative existence, i.e. the senses, the intellect and the ego and to turn the attention inwards towards the inner existence, to the eternal, beyond time and space and without any relative concepts in the now.

One of the obstacles to this transcendence is the mind and ego that want control and power over the individual consciousness. Because the mind constantly creates desires and needs that are directed towards the external relative existence, the attention can be kept there. The mind has been built up partly by its own experiences but also by influences from parents, relatives and friends, society as well as religious and political and religious ideas. Therefore, the mind cannot be said to be a source of the absolute truth but is a forum for relative i.e. changing ideas and attitudes that can vary greatly over a lifetime. The mind is nearly constantly activated in thoughts, reflections and emotions; it is the area of activity of the mind.

Of course, every human being must be engaged in the external existence and satisfy certain needs there, but it does not have to be at the expense of losing contact with the inner existence, with the real identity. It is possible to have undivided attention on both the mind and the Kingdom of Heaven at the same time. I.e. one has one foot in the Kingdom of Heaven and one foot on earth at the same time. It is a level of consciousness which means that one becomes aware of and uses the external relative existence and the absolute, eternal Kingdom of Heaven at the same time: to integrate the inner and the outer and become a whole person. In this state of consciousness self-sufficiency, happiness and peace arise. Being established on a level of consciousness where one is aware of the kingdom of God is the most important thing one can do during the time one lives on earth, everything else comes second. This should be the purpose of every human life on earth.

How shall I come in contact with the kingdom of God?

2. Jesus: But when you make your prayer, go into your private room, and, shutting the door, say a prayer to your Father in secret, and your Father, who sees in secret, will give you your reward. Matthew 6:7.

To make contact with "your father" in the present, Jesus gives a concrete suggestion how to do it. When the attention is directed towards the external existence, one is often bound by various activities there. It can therefore be good to withdraw to a place where attention can more easily be drawn inwards to "your father in secret". Jesus proposes to enter your private room, i.e. a place where there is silence and where peace can prevail. Peace arises when the attention is established in "The Father who sees in secret" which cannot be experienced through the senses or the intellect. The mind and intellect become obstacles instead of help when it comes to be aware of Consciousness. This is because the mind wants power and control over Consciousness. It is through the grace of God that union can take place.

It is first a matter of having a need to approach "the secret" and then find a suitable method that can bring attention there. The purpose is to never lose touch with "the secret" regardless of whether attention is also present in the relative existence. Using prayer to satisfy one's sensual needs becomes something that counteracts the contact with "Father in secret"; as such a prayer draws attention to the external sensual existence. To, without demands, but with a sincere desire and a need to unite with the "Father in the secret" in prayer or meditation, pay attention inwards provides the best conditions for a conscious association. An association that has always existed is and will be without duality, but which must be made aware.

What happens when we pray?

3. Jesus: And I say to you, make requests, and they will be answered; what you are searching for, you will get; when you give the sign, the door will be open to you. Luck 11:9.

Saints, mystics and spiritual preachers like Jesus and Buddha have always spoken of prayer and meditation as a spiritual aid. This creates an opportunity to let go of the activity of the mind and experience Consciousness, which results in absolute stillness, peace and being. There are many methods and techniques that work and that lead to awareness of Godconsciousness, but the most important thing of all is that there is a will and desire to leave the one-sided dominance of the mind and instead become aware of the Kingdom of Heaven. It is a waste of time to engage in prayer or meditation while

*thinking about pleasures or when the mind is preoccu-
pied with the desire for power and wealth. But once the
identification with and awareness of Consciousness is
established, this state is so satisfying and filled with bliss
and peace that all sensual satisfaction becomes completely uninteresting.*

**What are we to strive to achieve during our exis-
tence on earth?**

*4. Jesus: Make no store of wealth for yourselves on earth,
where it may be turned to dust by worms and weather,
and where thieves may come in by force and take it
away. But make a store for yourselves in heaven, where
it will not be turned to dust and where thieves do not
come in to take it away, for where your wealth is, there
will your heart be. Matthew 6:19-21.*

*In many people there is an inherent longing to be happy
and satisfied with life. This longing is expressed in the
form of a search for something that can bring satisfaction. It can be material welfare, good reputation and
worldly power. But all this gives only a temporary satisfaction and one must constantly search for something
new that can give satisfaction. These are the "treasures
here on earth." To "gather treasures in heaven" means to
turn one's attention inward to Consciousness. Then you
experience self-sufficiency, i.e. to be happy and satis-*

fied with being in what is in the present. This state of Consciousness is the true spiritual identity. There is then nothing that you need to strive for or try to achieve. This does not mean that one should stop acting and be active in the external life that constantly needs to be changed, improved and maintained. When you leave earthly life, you cannot take with you the worldly material treasures that you have collected on earth, while the spiritual treasures that you have acquired remain as knowledge and awareness.

But there is so much that needs to be done, we need to work for the bread, when are we going to have time for prayer and meditation?

But there is so much that needs to be done, we need to work for the bread, when are we going to have time for prayer and meditation?

5. Jesus: But let your first care be for his kingdom and his righteousness; and all these other things will be given to you in addition. Matthew 6:33.

"His kingdom" is the inner spiritual Kingdom of Heaven or the Consciousness which is also everything, i.e. all things, ground. To be established there, means to be sup-ported and provide for by what has the total control and power over the entire relative existence, i.e. God's

consciousness. What is called it is irrelevant as it is impossible to define it as an object. There are few words that have as many prejudices and definitions as the word God. Often one associates God with something that exists in external existence and from which one is separated. Therefore, the Kingdom of Heaven or Consciousness is a better word in this context as there is no doubt that Consciousness is within us in the inner existence.

When you are established in "his kingdom", what is needed in the present comes automatically, without any effort or resistance and you live a righteous life completely naturally without making an effort or following any established rules of life. Life is then without resistance and based on being in harmony with Consciousness. You then do not have to strive to get what you need. The knowledge and necessary experiences, both good and bad, come when they are needed, you do not have to look for them anymore. Life then becomes focused on being in the Consciousness instead of doing in the relative existence. You feel self-sufficient and peaceful.

What does it mean to be in harmony with life?
6. Jesus: He who has the desire to keep his life will have it taken from him, and he who gives up his life because of me will have it given back to him. Matthew 10:39.

Life is not what we have but what we are. Once we have realized this, we understand that life exists in the present, in eternity. When you associate the mind and ego with life, life becomes something temporary that involves a constant struggle against death. It is believed that life is something that only exists between the date of birth and the date of death. When you can let the attention go from the mind and ego to Consiousness, you are no longer bound by the relative time dimension of life. Then you can be aware from this level of consciousness that life is eternal. If you try to cling to the life situation between birth and death, it is the mind and ego that you cling to. You will lose this when you die, but the one who during life is not bound by the mind and ego is aware of eternal life. When there is no longer a desire for the world, which was previously the primary and in focus to be satisfied, one can say that one has lost the worldly outer life but at the same time found the real eternal life and thus one's true identity.

What attitude should we have to experience the Kingdom of Heaven?

7. Jesus: Truly, I say to you, If you do not have a change of heart and become like little children, you will not go into the kingdom of heaven. Whoever, then, will make himself as low as this little child, the same is the greatest in the kingdom of heaven. Matthew 18:3-4.

From the beginning, a child is naturally identified with its true nature and rooted in the present. This state of awareness is the portal to the Kingdom of Heaven. The child is taught and educated by his surroundings to build an ego identity that judges and judges according to the norms that the environment has created. It is parents, peers, schools, authorities, politicians and society in general with media influence in the form of music, film, television, as well as religion and politics that help to build a fictional picture of life. This one-sided fictional picture of life can become an obstacle if one wants to maintain the identification with one's true nature. In order to be able to "repent", one must keep the attention on Consciousness, i.e. be in the Kingdom of Heaven. Of course, we must also be able to live with the fictitious ego identification to be able to navigate in the relative existence, but at the same time we must be able to let the attention be in the Kingdom of Heaven, i.e. have simultaneous attention to the mind and ego on the one hand and the Kingdom of Heaven on the other side. You need to have one foot in the relative world and one in the absolute Consciousness, i.e. in the Kingdom of Heaven. Young children's attitudes towards their environment are not intellectual and judgmental according to learned norms. Of course, young children must learn certain rules of conduct in order not to harm themselves or others. These guidelines are helpful until the day when they have the opportunity to receive insight and awareness of what is right and wrong in the present. This happens when they have become more aware of life as a whole. In many religions it is said that one should fear God if one does not live by certain rules of life, if one does not do so one should be punished by God. This assumption does not come from God but from the human mind and intellect. You can see that an aggressive person wants to punish and take revenge. This is a function of the human dysfunctional ego. It is therefore believed that God works in the same way. But God is conscious, God does not need to punish, it is the unconscious and ignorance that punishes itself. Suffering is a function of unconsciousness and ignorance. A conscious person has no need to judge and punish. God wants man to become aware and gain knowledge about life and the whole of existence. From this state of consciousness arises the unconditional altruistic love that is based on compassion. The intellectually educated man has acquired a definite learned conception of existence which sometimes acts as an obstacle when it comes to bringing attention to Consciousness. The intellectual acts as a filter and thus an obstacle to be aware of Consciousness. There is no way to be aware of Consciousness through the mind and ego. As long as the attention is present in the mind, one identifies with the mind and the external existence. The identity is then formed by material possessions, power, social status and different roles that one takes on. Since

awareness can be present in Consciousness, one has the opportunity to observe the temporarily created external identity. One then experiences that this identity is not real but temporarily created to suit the needs of the ego. It is then that the real, eternal, unchanging inner identity observes this illusory, transient, unreal outer identity.

If we cannot experience the Kingdom of Heaven here and now, maybe we can experience the Kingdom of Heaven when we die?

8. Jesus: Truly I say to you, whatever things are fixed by you on earth will be fixed in heaven: and whatever you make free on earth will be made free in heaven. Matthew 18:18.

The wisdom that a person acquires during life on earth continues to be conscious even when one has left his earthly life. Knowledge does not come automatically just because one has left the earth. Knowledge and wisdom must be obtained during the life of the earth. Saints and wise men arise on earth as butterflies that are freed from the cocoon of the mind and ego. This liberation that arises when one realizes one's true identity must take place during life on earth. When one is aware of the Kingdom of Heaven, knowledge and wisdom are automatically released to suit what is happening in the present. This knowledge is not created by the intellect and

*memory, but arises spontaneously as a reality-adapted
insight. So it is not the case that if you are unhappy on
earth, you will automatically be happy in heaven when
you die. It is a mistake to think that suicide solves the
problem of suffering, quite the opposite. It is on earth
that one can realize oneself and find one's true identity
and not after death has occurred.*

**How should we relate to our ego, which has the
ambition to assert itself at the expense of others and
show its excellence?**

*9. Jesus: So the last will be first and the first last. But
if anyone has a desire to become great among you, let
him be your servant and whoever has a desire to be first
among you, let him take the lowest place: even as the
Son of man did not come to have servants, but to be
a servant, and to give his life for the salvation of men.
Matt 20: 16, 20:26-28.*

*The ego is a surrogate identity that dominates until the
identity with Consciousness is established. Then the ego
has only a practical function to fulfill, i.e. to be helpful and to be a tool for navigating worldly existence.
Living with a strong egoidentity results in perceived
duality with life. I.e. through the dualistic individuality
the ego can exist separated. As attention is established
at the level of the mind, a conceptual assessment of*

what is happening takes place and the mind often acts after the assessment. The nature of the mind and ego includes asserting oneself, often at the expense of the environment. Many sensory activities therefore involve asserting oneself and showing the excellence of the ego. These sensory activities then result in physical activities that will result in the creation of something that has the task of emphasizing the ego. It is often important that you can assert yourself by being the best, first, most beautiful or being the most intelligent. Companies, schools, political parties, religious organizations, sports associations are often hierarchically structured in terms of power and position. These structures suit the ego that strives and has a desire for wealth, power and position. It is important to assert oneself in order to be prominent in these hierarchical structures. Being first and foremost becomes a prerequisite for being able to defeat opponents who have the same goals, desires and desires. These organizations act as perfect breeding grounds for the ego and can cause immense suffering to those who fail to assert themselves. This is what Jesus meant when he said; "There will come a time when the first will be the last and the last will be the first." The first are those who only have a desire for worldly influence, i.e. wealth, power and position. Because the attention is completely focused on the worldly, they will be completely blinded and preoccupied with their abilities and sensual desire and miss the opportunity to experience the spiritual

*dimension, i.e. Consciousness, while one who can be
awake and present in Consciousness often prioritizes
to attain spiritual insight and experience harmony
and peace. These individuals are automatically high-
lighted by life without any struggle or intellectual effort
and without having to push themselves forward at the
expense of their fellow human beings. He who can be
present in the Consciousness is not lost in duality and
diversity but in unity with existence. He does not have
to assert itself by striving to be first and foremost. By
being without resistance and effort, life works for him,
and then he who is in unity with life becomes first and
foremost successful without striving for it. You do not
have to strive to become something or someone, but you
do what is to be done in the present. Naturally, you are
who you are and one with the Master of the universe
without striving for it. One can be the servant and slave
of others and at the same time the Master.*

*10. Jesus continued: For every man who gives himself
a high place will be put down, but he who takes a low
place will be lifted up. Luk 14:11.*

*Since a person's awareness is dominated by the ego, it is
only natural to want to exalt oneself and show that one
is something special. How this is received by the environment depends on the level of awareness of the environ-*

*ment. To assert oneself at the expense of the environ-
ment is often stimulating for the ego, but less pleasant
for the egos that are affected, and conflicts often arise.
He who exalts himself excessively can often be humiliat-
ed and ridiculed by those around him. Someone who is
humble and does not allow himself to be controlled by
the ego is often respected by those around him. This is
because the one who is conscious and humble is often in
the hands of the factor that has power and insight into
the total existence.*

How to best apply your teaching?

*11. Jesus: If any man has the desire to come after me, let
him give up all other desires, and take up his cross and
come after me. Mark 8:34.*

*A spiritual master, you must "deny yourself", i.e. take
the attention from the mind and ego and become aware
of Consciousness and "take your cross and follow me,"
i.e., to accept life as it is, and cannot be in any other
way than it is, even if it involves suffering and hardship.
Finding your spiritual origin can mean going through
both difficulties and joy. It may be necessary for a
spiritual awakening to realize that worldly existence is
not always a life in paradise but is also suffering and
problems. By realizing this, it becomes a natural step
to turn attention inward toward Consciousness. In this*

way, suffering has also had a function to fill in life, i.e. be a guide to the real eternal life and the true identity.

Where should I follow you?

12. Jesus: My kingdom is not of this world. Joh 18:36.

The kingdom to which Jesus refers is not a worldly place but a spiritual kingdom or state of consciousness. It is the Kingdom of Heaven which is the fourth state of consciousness besides wakefulness, sleep and dream. It can be experienced if you are awake and present. When Jesus says "this world", he means the relatively changing existence that has a beginning and an end, which is dependent on experiences from the five senses and from the intellect. The mind is dependent on thoughts and feelings for its existence. It is dualistic in nature and its ego lives in an illusory separated state in relation to other egos.

Jesus was completely focused on man, developing spiritually to become aware of the Kingdom of Heaven and thus integrated with it.

But how will it go?

13. Jesus: You are to keep watch: because you are not certain when the master of the house is coming! Mark 13:35.

To be awake means to be aware and present. "Lord of the house" in this context is Godconsciousness which is the reality and the origin of everything. When the master of the house comes you have to be awake, you never know when this will happen. It is not an event that the mind can plan for or decide over. There is nothing you can do, other than to be present and awake. This happens when you are ripe for it, in the same way as when you harvest the grapes when they are ripe, if you do it too early the wine becomes sour and undrinkable. Many people are not mature and thus have not wake up, but live in a kind of dream sleep when it comes to the inner life. What is required is that you wake up and become consciously present and thereby become aware of the Kingdom of Heaven, i.e. Consciousness and his identity with it. This can happen spontaneously, all of a sudden without any effort or intellectual commitment. You often experience an inner peace and security in yourself, which is also accompanied by a clear vision. You can then experience that the various pieces of the puzzle that you have in the current life situation fall into place and you can see a higher meaning with everything that is and has happened.

What happens then, is there anything that needs to be done to get to the kingdom of God?

14. Jesus: Truly, I say to you, without a new birth no man is able to see the kingdom of God. John 3:3.

To be born again does not mean, in this context, to be born in a new body but in a new state of awareness. To turn attention inward and be in a state of awareness where one is aware of the Kingdom of Heaven. To be present in Consciousness and thus have the ability to observe and see the mind and the relative existence, i.e. see the manifested kingdom of God. As long as one is identified with the mind and the relative existence, one cannot see the Consciousness as one is limited by the relative existence. You cannot see something as you are, in the same way that you cannot see the Consciousness when you are Consciousness. It can be said that the first birth is the birth of the body and mind and the second birth is a rebirth in Consciousness, i.e. in the kingdom of God.

What does it mean to be born again?

15. Jesus: Truly, I say to you, If a man's birth is not from water and from the Spirit, it is not possible for him to go into the kingdom of God. That which has birth from the flesh is flesh, and that which has birth from the Spirit is spirit. John 3:5-6.

The Spirit or the kingdom of God and life is the eternal unmanifested that creates maintains and breaks down the manifested material existence. There is nothing or any place where the kingdom of God or life does not exist, it is present everywhere. The smallest particle is

Godconsciousness and is controlled by Godconscious-
ness and it controls every single living cell. What we
call material existence cannot exist separately from the
Godconsciousness. To "enter the kingdom of God" one
must become aware of the kingdom of God. This is to be
born in a new state of awareness where the mind does
not dominate the attention.

In many religions, water has become a link between
man and God. You are baptized in water and you wash
away your sins symbolically with water. To be born in
the flesh is to take up residence in the world through a
living organism. It is the Spirit that incarnates on earth
in a living organism in order to develop and eventually
become aware of itself, i.e. aware of Consciousness. This
incarnation is a completely mental and spiritual process,
where even the so-called physical body is mental, i.e. the
body can only be experienced mentally with the help of
the five senses.

**How can one be freed from problems and suffering
and be able to live rooted in God?**
16. Jesus: I am the door: if any man goes in through me
he will have salvation. John 10:9.

There are many gates or portals to the Kingdom of
Heaven. The important thing is that you have a desire to

*be aware in the Kingdom of Heaven or Consciousness.
Once you have decided to pay attention there, you have
to open the gate. Opening the gate and entering can be
a process that can be difficult and cumbersome if you
are not ready for it. The mind and ego want to maintain
awareness in the world where there is material success,
power and pleasures. If you have unsatisfied desires,
they want to attract attention and make man forget the
Kingdom of Heaven, which does not offer the worldly
pleasures but a presence in Consciousness. Constantly
striving to be happy ultimately gives the experience
that in the sensual world there is no permanent state
of happiness and self-sufficiency. Then you are ready to
enter through the gate to the Kingdom of Heaven where
permanent peace and self-sufficiency prevail, where
Consciousness is. When you are mature, it is easy and
obvious to enter through the gate. In Consciousness one
is liberated from suffering and the sensual desires.*

Why is it that you can say that you are the gate to God?

*17. Jesus: I and my Father are one. The Father is in me
and I am in the Father. John 10:30 and 38.*

*To be present in Godconsciousness, i.e. in the Father,
means that there is no duality. "I and the Father are
one", means that it is a non-dualistic relationship*

between Jesus and the Father. Since the identification is not with the mind and ego but with God- consciousness , there has been a change of identity from an illusory state to a real identity. This union means the final completion. There is nothing more to develop, no way to tread when awareness is present in the Father.

How can we know what is right and proper?
18. Jesus: when he, the Spirit of true knowledge, has come, he will be your guide into all true knowledge. John 16:13.

Truth or wisdom comes as insights to the one who is consciously present in the Consciousness. It is intuitive knowledge that comes directly without having to be judged by the mind. It does not have to be constructed by the intellect. When the truth comes, it is perceived as completely obvious and does not need to be questioned. It is revealed there and the task of the mind is to communicate it verbally, in writing or keep it in memory.

Is the purpose that everyone should be perfect and become one with the Father? What do you say to the Father about this?
19. Jesus: Holy Father, keep them in your name which you have given to me, so that they may be one even as we are one. John 17:11.

And;

The glory which you have e given to me I have given to them, so that they may be one even as we are one. John 17:22.

In these statements Jesus explains the purpose of life, i.e. to be perfected and become one with the Father. It is predestined that everyone should become aware of Consciousness. God is "omnipresent" in everything, thus everything and everyone is already one with Consciousness. Nothing can be separated from Consciousness. To be perfected is to become aware and present in Consciousness, to have a non-dualistic identity. It is not just the gift of a select few spiritual masters. The masters who are consciously present in the source of existence, i.e. Consciousness, has understood that it is the purpose of life to be united and aware of this relationship. They have been ahead of their fellow human beings in terms of time when it comes to living in this state of awareness. They have tried to help by being role models and guides. The problem is that from the mind it is not possible to experience this relationship. From the mind, one can gain knowledge as many times as you like about this relationship without the association taking place. It is not the task of the mind and intellect to become aware of Consciousness. They are tools in the relative existence. The non-dualistic identity arises when there is the pre-condition and maturity for it.

How can we be empowered to undergo this spiritual transformation?

20. Jesus: You will have power, when the Holy Spirit has come on you. Apg 1:8.

The Holy Spirit i.e. Consciousness is fundamental to everything and everyone. Even if you do not experience any contact, the Holy Spirit is there as the maintainer. If the Holy Spirit were not there, both material and spiritual existence would immediately collapse and cease to exist. Most people live life without conscious contact with the Holy Spirit who is life itself. But then one can pay attention to the Holy Spirit, ie. being present in this state of consciousness, it results in being filled with the power of the spirit both physically and spiritually. You no longer need to believe in the Holy Spirit. The Holy Spirit is the life force that is the source of all life. It is this power that gives you peace when it comes over you. Peace is complete, when you experience it you no longer need to search for more peace. When "the Holy Spirit comes upon you", this can mean that you are ready to receive knowledge through intuition. The acquisition of knowledge via intuition takes place without duality, ie. as an absolute truth. Knowledge at this level is expe-rienced directly without the logical intervention of the intellect. This intuitive experience provides insights on a conscious level, which is perceived as obvious logic. It is usually experienced that knowledge comes as a "clear vision" or "a flash from clear skies". It is experienced as being received without any interference from the mind and intellect. Knowledge is related to what one needs to know in the present and has the ability to understand. With the help of thoughts, the individual captures the knowledge that comes as an impulse or feeling. It feels like an inner certainty that can be clothed with words. Of course, it becomes relatively colored when you then try to express it verbally or in writing.

How will God give us help and knowledge?

21. Jesus: The Helper, the Holy Spirit, whom the Father will send in my name, will be your teacher in all things and will put you in mind of everything I have said to you. May peace be with you; my peace I give to you. John 14:26-27.

When the master can't be present physically, the Holy Spirit is always there and reminds and shows the way. If you then have your attention directed inwards, appropriate wisdom comes into the present. Living in such conditions brings invincibility and peace. The ignorance of worldly existence has then lost its power in favor of the spiritual consciousness which gives wisdom and peace. The Holy Ghost gives wisdom to him who is ready to receive it. With the help of knowledge, we describe life. Knowledge also provides an opportunity for understanding life. This understanding enables the ability to create contexts and relationships. The way to obtain knowledge depends on the state of awareness we are in. At the level of the mind, the acquisition of knowledge takes place via the intellect and when there is awareness of Consciousness, i.e. the kingdom of heaven and the Holy Spirit, it can often happen through intuition, knowledge is then often called wisdom.

The acquisition of knowledge via the intellect often takes place through an external source, via a book, another human being or through sensory perception of existence. At this level, knowledge becomes relative information. It is then dependent on time and space, i.e. the environment and spirit of the time that exists in the present. The intellect arranges and structures the information logically and creates new information on the basis of the old one. It is a communication between old experiences or information and the intellect's ability to draw conclusions in the present. At this level, the intellect is a creator of relative knowledge.

When will everything be revealed?
22. Jesus: The Father's imperial rule is inside you and outside you. When you know yourselves, then you will be known, and you will understand that you are

children of the living Father. But if you do not know yourselves, then you live in poverty, and you are the poverty. Thomas 3.

The kingdom of heaven is eternal and infinite. This space that is independent of time and space can be experienced. When the awareness is there, one can experience the individual awareness united with the collective Consciousness, with the Father. The association is there regardless of what level of awareness prevails, i.e. if one sleeps, dreams, or is active and awake in external existence. When you feel yourself, i.e. the true identity, this means that you also feels and is constantly present in the Father. You do not then live in spiritual poverty. Everything is then revealed.

Ultimately, it is always Consciousness that is the basis of everything and that governs life even if we are not aware of it. When we do not have contact with Consciousness, we are not aware of this relationship. Then we can act and be in life in a way that results in disharmony and negativity and thus suffering. When awareness is present in Consciousness', it is the presence in the now that counts. Then there is no pre-determined plan for dealing with existence. Insights then constantly arise and at the same time impulses for activity. Of course, this does not mean that life cannot be planned. For example, it is obvious that we have to sow in the spring so that we can harvest in the autumn. What is described here is a state of consciousness that does not allow for any compromises with the mind. For those who are not yet permanently established in this state, it is still possible to compromise. Sometimes the mind controls with its relative and limited way of looking at life and sometimes the attention is on the unlimited Consciousness which then provides unlimited possibilities.

Is there any dualism when everything is revealed?
23. Jesus: When you make the two into one, and when you make the inner like the outer and the outer like the inner, and the upper like the lower, and when you make male and female into a single one, so that the male will not be male nor the female be female Thomas 22.

When there is no dualism, when the one who observes and what is observed is one, when one is self-sufficient and there is no desire to have or any need to supplement with anything, then there is only Consciousness. There is then no reason to be identified with the individual sense awareness and to hold on to an identity as a man or woman. The identity is then not individual but is then the conscious witnessing Consciousness. However, the physical senses, the intellect and the ego are still used as tools and aids to navigate life, but there is no longer ego identification with the mind. You are then invincible, i.e. the mind awareness then no longer has the opportunity to dominate and control. At this level of awareness, one is dead based on the individual conceptual level of the mind, but totally present and conscious in Consciousness and automatically and without resistance, one is in the Kingdom of Heaven.

Does the Father have both a changing and an unchanging state?

24. Jesus: What is the evidence of your Father in you? It is motion and rest. Thomas 50.

The relative worldly existence is in constant motion, while the absolute spiritual existence is in constant rest. These two states, movement and rest, are not incompatible. A human being can be present in these two states at the same time and has then realized the whole of life, i.e. active and acting in the world and at the same time aware and resting in Consciousness. This condition is a sign that one is aware of the union with the Father. The father is beyond all concepts, i.e. can not be limited by a conceptual description and is thus neither identified with the movement nor with rest and stillness, but is simultaneously present in both states.

The absolute immutable Godconsciousness is the basis of relative existence, and both parts are interdependent in order for existence to be. They are opposites of each other but at the same time they cannot exist separately. To be able to experience and be aware of the relative and the absolute at the same time means unity consciousness, this is the perfect state of Consciousness. The state of consciousness "ubiquitous" is an experience in the relative existence that must not be confused with unity Consciousness. When Consciousness is inactive and not in motion, can this characterize awareness to be in stillness and in inner peace. To be simultaneously aware of the relative changing existence means to be completely in unity with what is, i.e. the totality of existence. Silence and stillness then also go hand in hand with activity and mind presence. Self-realization is then a reality. Reality and truth are then established.

What is the difference between one who is consciously united with the Father and one who is not conscious of the Father?
25. Jesus: If one is whole, one will be filled with light, but if one is divided, one will be filled with darkness."
Thomas 61.

When one has realized the whole of life and is consciously united with the Father, one can be called enlightened, i.e. awake and filled with an inner light. Since the dysfunctional ego has power over a person's aware-

ness, there is the opposite, division and duality that give a mental darkness. The closer you get to the light, the more distant the darkness becomes.

How and when do you find the Kingdom?

26. Jesus: If you do not fast from the world, you will not find the Father's domain. Thomas 27.

If one does not refrain from desire for the world, attention will be directed towards the world and one has then limited the possibility of being aware of the Father or Consciousness, at the same time. To renounce the world altogether is not the way to the Father. One should be able to live in the world and use the world without being dependent and bound by it. If one has no desire for the world, the world has no power. But even if one has no desire for the world, this is not certain to the Kingdom of Heaven opens automatically. One can never know when the presence in Consciousness' becomes conscious. If the mind has expectations and desires to become conscious, this does not automatically give access, it can instead have the opposite effect. I.e. attention stays at the level of awareness of the mind. However, if one experiences that happiness and peace are greater in Consciousness than in the level of awareness of the mind, attention is automatically drawn to it.

The mind, ego and intellect create individual desires and needs that must be satisfied in the future. It is these desires and needs that create the individual existence. Since they no longer arise, there is also no seed for further individual existence. Memory, intellect, senses and ego enable the existence of the mind. Today's prevailing consciousness means that people are firmly rooted in the mind and the driving force is then the desire for pleasure, wealth, power and position. The goal of attention becomes the aspects of the mind that provide the most satisfaction and security for the moment. It becomes a constant pursuit of sensual satisfaction. It is a waste of time to engage in prayer or meditation while thinking about pleasures or having thoughts that are preoccupied with the desire for power and wealth. But once the identification with Consciousness is established, this state is so satisfying and filled with bliss and peace that all sensual satisfaction becomes completely uninteresting.

Where can one see the kingdom of the Father?
27. Jesus: The Father's imperial rule is spread out upon the earth and people don't see it. Thomas 113.

The Father´s rule is not a physical kingdom that you can see, but a kingdom that you can be aware of, if you are present and conscious. There is no realm that you can observe as you cannot observe something that you are. It is a non-dualistic relationship, i.e. no relationship.

As long as one is in love with the world and has the attention in the world, one is not present in Consciousness, but one can never be separated from Consciousness. There are many levels of awareness in the relative existence and the degree of awareness varies, but at the absolute level there is only Consciousness i.e. "The Kingdom of the Father". The Kingdom is everywhere and is the basis of everything, but it is up to each individual to become aware of it and identify with it. It is not enough to believe that it exists. Being able to be constantly present in the "Kingdom of the Father" means, you can realize awareness of Consciousness, which is the highest purpose of life.

What do you have to do, to be able to receive Jesus?
28. Jesus: If any man has a desire to come after me, let him give up all, and take up his cross every day, and come after me. Lukas 9:23.

Jesus was established in Consciousness. Following Jesus means establishing oneself in this state of spiritual consciousness. In order to receive this state of Consciousness, it is necessary to renounce or give up the mind and ego's desire for power over awareness in order to thereby draw attention to Consciousness. The awareness is then not a slave to the mind and ego. To renounce the mind and ego does not mean that one must renounce the

*world and become a monk or a nun. What is import-
ant is the relationship to the mind and the ego and the
material world. Not identifying with the ego and the
material world can be achieved through undivided
attention, i.e. that one pays attention at the same time
to both the material and the spiritual existence, i.e., on
the mind and at the same time on the Consciousness.
This can be experienced as a struggle when both the
ego and the world want attention to gain power over
consciousness. If you are not in love with the worldly, i.e.
do not have a desire for power and position as well as
material possessions to elevate the ego-identity, one can
have a witnessing attitude in relation to the ego and the
world. There will then be no bonding and there will be
no struggle or resistance.*

*To allow the conscious attention to leave the relative
time-bound conceptual existence and to unilaterally pay
attention to the absolute eternal unbound existence is
called to transcend. This transcendence can occur from
any relative state of consciousness. Then awareness is
totally integrated with Consciousness and the individual
is no longer active. This happens when death occurs. It
can also occur during a certain period of time during
prayer or meditation.*

I often feel worried about the future, how should I relate to it?

29 Jesus: Then have no care for tomorrow: tomorrow will take care of itself. Take the trouble of the day as it comes. Matthew 6:34.

Tomorrow is not reality but only a fantasy in the human mind. Neither the past nor the future are real, only the present is real. Real life always takes place in the present. The present is an eternal arena for activity and non-activity. The mind often creates worries and anxieties that are attributed to the future or have anxiety about what has happened in the past. It is completely unnecessary to create more worries and suffering than what exists in the now. Always be focused on what is happening, and be present in the now.

Even the past can give uneasy thoughts and anxiety, how should one relate to it?

30. Jesus: No man, having put his hand to the plough and looking back, is good enough for the kingdom of God. Luke 9:62.

The Kingdom of God exists only in the present; he who lives in the past puts attention there and misses the present where The Kingdom of God exists. Therefore, life becomes more real if you can be consciously present in

*what is happening in the now. Of course, there are men-
tally stored in memory things that have happened in
the past and it can be difficult to turn off the memory of
these experiences. Sometimes it can be positive to have
certain experiences that can be helpful in the present,
but some destructive experiences can become an obstacle and problem in the present if they only contribute
with negativity such as, aggression, hatred, and revenge.
One can enter the Kingdom by being consciously aware
in the present.*

**But to be successful in this life, you have to work
hard and do your duty and then you also have to
plan for this to become a reality in the future!**

*31. Jesus: For this reason I say to you, take no thought
for your life, about what food you will take, or for your
body, how it may be clothed. Is not life more than food,
and the body than its clothing? Give thought to the ravens; they do not put seeds into the earth, or get together
grain; they have no store-houses or buildings; and God
gives them their food: of how much greater value are
you than the birds! But let your chief care be for his
kingdom, and these other things will be given to you in
addition. Luke. 12:22-23, 31.*

*For many, life becomes a concern when they pay atten-
tion to the future. There is almost always something*

to worry about. There is a fear of the future and one must guard against the ominous future. This state of consciousness often leads to mental illness in the form of anxiety, worry and depression. To be able to take life as it comes and to accept life as it is, is the best prerequisite for contact with Consciousness. The prerequisite for being able to accept life as it is, is the realization that life can not be in any other way than as it is right now. By being in Consciousness, you do not have to worry; life takes care of the individual and ensures that it gets what is needed. The most important thing is to be present in Consciousness, and then help with worldly existence will come. Help does not always come as the ego has intended, completely new circumstances can arise in the present.

32. Jesus continued: Don't fret, from morning to evening and from evening to morning, about what you're going to wear. Thomas 36.

For one who is one with the Consciousness or the Kingdom, there are no unnecessary worries in life, what is in the present is accepted and received without conflict when one knows that it can not be in any other way than what is in the present. Living without conflict with life is a must to be able to be in the Kingdom. To live in conflict is to live in duality with existence. Of course, there are differences and these must be tolerated and accepted without conflicts. The whole of relative worldly existence consists of differences. The relative changing existence includes both the inner and the outer existence. The inner existence is comprised of feelings, sensations, and thoughts, all of which are mental experiences. External existence is what the sense organs convey and that is also a mental consciousness. To witness the relative existence is to be aware in the present. There are then no worries for tomorrow as tomorrow is not a reality in the present but only a fiction.

But I do not really understand, this life I live, is the most important thing I have, I have to plan and make sure it will be as good as possible for me!
33. Jesus: He who is in love with life will have it taken from him; and he who has no care for his life in this world will keep it forever and ever. John 12:25.

Life is eternal and cannot be lost, but he who loses "his life" does not lose life without the identification with his life situation and the relative mind and ego. Losing one's ego identification means that there is no longer a need for the ego to have power over Consciousness. When this need no longer exists, the ego can no longer rule over Consciousness. When this happens, attention can be drawn to the Consciousness without resistance. He who can be aware of Consciousness has received the highest that a human being can achieve, i.e. conscious contact with life, with Consciousness, with the Kingdom of God.

How should I treat people who want to hurt me?
34. Jesus: Do not make use of force against an evil man; but to him who gives you a blow on the right side of your face let the left be turned. Matt 5:39.

He who is established and aware of Consciousness is not bound to the duality of existence. The ego then experiences no conflict or struggle to be able to assert itself. An assessment is made of the situation that arises but is not judged. Going to attack is because you have made an assessment that results in an aggression that leads to hatred and revenge. All human conflicts that lead to violence, i.e. to hatred and revenge are due to the aggression being given the opportunity to manifest itself. Often there is a choice between aggression or humility and compassion. Instead of letting the aggression start automatically, it can be very helpful to make an impact assessment in order to be consciously present in a humble and compassionate level of awareness. You let mercy go before justice. This does not mean that one should be exposed to unnecessary risks, but sometimes such an act as "turning the other cheek" can evoke awareness in the person who strikes. Aggressiveness is best disarmed by non-aggression, i.e. compassion and love. Instead of

*giving birth to aggression, you give birth to compassion
and love.*

If I'm attacked by a malicious person, how should I act?

*35. Jesus: Put up your sword again into its place: for
all those who take the sword will come to death by the
sword. Matt 26:52.*

*The negativity and aggression that one sends out will
affect oneself sooner or later. Using force is not a permanent solution. If you solve a problem in the present with
violence, the result of this action will affect so that a
new problem arises. It is often said that violence breeds
violence, aggression often results in hatred and revenge.
This spiral of violence must be broken in some way.
When the dysfunctional ego is given space in a person's
consciousness, morality and compassionate behavior are
often neglected. Compassion does not become present
in consciousness when aggression takes over. On an
individual level, it is said that the individual acts in
affect. It is then that acts of violence such as assault, and
murder occur. But a conflict does not always go as far
as physical violence. Conflicts that arise between people
often lead to mental battles. Then it is argumentation
with words that are the weapons. There are different
ideologies; political or religious that are pitted against*

each other. If the person is not tolerant, anger or aggression occurs and it often ends with personal attacks. This behavior is on an individual level but can also occur on a collective level. It can then be a certain group or association of individuals who fight against each other for power; politically, religiously or ideologically. In exactly the same way, it is with states that come into conflict with each other. If there is no awareness that is characterized by tolerance and compassion, there are no conditions for constructive solutions for both parties. Then a conflict often arises between countries. There will then be a war with weapons. At a collective level, it is the country's consciousness that shapes the country's leaders. Countries with primitive and low consciousness get leaders who are prone to personal exercise of power and corruption. These leaders let their personal ego and greed take precedence over the wellbeing of the people. Problems arise for these leaders as people's awareness is raised to the point that they realize that freedom is being curtailed and that the country's leaders are abusing their power both economically and politically. Sometimes circumstances arise that we believe we can not influence. We blame ourselves for being victims of prevailing circumstances. But according to the law of cause and effect, it is always we ourselves who have created the conditions for what we experience in the present. The law of cause and effect works educatively in the school of life in a concrete way. The spiritual insights provide direct knowledge on both a physically concrete level and an abstract mental level. Existence in the present cannot be different from what it is. What we experience in the present is often a reflection of what we have created in the past. History repeats itself until we have learned our lessons. We may have wishes that it would be different from what it is, but these wishes must be realized in the present in order for them to become reality. By observing and accepting life as it is, we can have a relationship to life without duality and conflict regardless of whether what we experience is light or dark. This starting point, which means that we are not in conflict with existence, is the path to spiritual liberation and the end of the mind's dominance over awareness. When the love of almost is established through presence in Consciousness, no acts of aggression arise and there is then no need to hate and take revenge or to exercise oppression of power. Then you do not have to use the sword and then you do not risk being killed by a sword.

36. Jesus: but I say to you, have love for those who are against you, and make prayer for those who are cruel to you. Matt 5:44.

Unconditional love neutralizes conflict and resistance. When one can realize that the root of conflicts is uncon-

*sciousness and ignorance, one can experience com-
passion and thus forgive one's enemies and those who
persecute and pray for them. When praying, one can
take attention from the worldly existence to the spiritual
existence and neutralize negativity. The enemy and the
one who pursues you are basically the same as you, i.e.
Consciousness. But it is required that this level of awareness, that can forgive, is established in pure Consciousness. Then forgiveness also becomes a prayer that affects
directly from a deeper level of awareness. Loving your
enemies is an impossibility if you have not mentally left
your ego. The ego is totally dualistic and does not have
the ability to realize that everything in life is connected.
Therefore, conscious presence must be in Consciousness
in order to love one's enemies and those who persecute.*

Why is it wrong to judge others?

*37. Jesus; why do you take note of the grain of dust in
your brother's eye, but take no note of the bit of wood
which is in your eye? Matt 7:3.*

*As long as the mind and ego dominate awareness, the
ego would rather emphasize the faults and shortcomings
of others than its own faults and shortcomings. It is a
way of strengthening one's own identity, which is based
on the ego and its excellence. Then it is also easier to
give advice to others than to take advice from others.*

It is therefore important that you gain self-insight and can observe the mind. When you can do that, you also realize that you do not have to identify with who you pretend to be but with who you are, i.e. not with the mind and the ego but with the Consciousness. There is then no need to judge the surroundings. You then accept the environment as it is, at the same time as you realize that it cannot be in any other way than it is. There is then no need to judge.

How should I behave when people around me do not understand what is sacred and true?
38. Jesus: Do not give that which is holy to the dogs, or put your jewels before pigs, for fear that they will be crushed under foot by the pigs whose attack will then be made against you. Matthew 7:6.

Knowledge is a tool that you can use when navigating your way in life. Some knowledge is gained through the mind and intellect through learning. There is also knowledge that does not pass through the intellect, mind and memory but comes directly from Conscious-ness . This knowledge or wisdom is experienced as an obvious insight, an intuition that emerges at the right time. Knowledge comes when you are mature enough to receive it. If you are not mature for it, you cannot un-derstand it and not use it. The knowledge then becomes like "put your jewels before pigs". If the knowledge ends up in fertile soil, it will germinate and develop into a beautiful plant that is rooted in the fertile soil. There is no reason to spread knowledge to the environment if it is not interested and not mature for it.

Governments do not always want to act in the way that I think is true and right, how should one behave then? 39. Jesus: Give to Caesar the things which are Caesar's, and to God the things which are God's. Matthew 22:21. To live aware of Consciousness, does not mean that one must renounce the world. There are societal duties that must continue to be performed, e.g. pay taxes. But the awareness of Consciousness does not have to disappear with acting in the world. The spiritual and the secular are integrated, if you have undivided attention you are not bound and enslaved by the world. One can have a conscious presence at the same time on both the worldly and the spiritual plane.

What is the most important approach to fellow human beings?

40. Jesus: All those things, then, which you would have men do to you, even so do you to them. Matthew 7:12. Morality and ethics are the guidelines that influence an individual's behavior. They are intimately connected to the time and environment in which the individual lives.

Many of the religions refer to the "golden rule", which says "do unto others what you want others to do to you". This golden rule is found in all major religions. It is a "guideline" which means that one can make an assessment by observing oneself. If you yourself want to be treated in an honest and dignified way, then you must also treat your neighbor in an honest and dignified way. It is a simple rule based on the fact that we are relatively similar at heart and react in much the same way. It is also often said that; "As you know yourself, you know others".

How can one know that a human being is true and trustworthy?

41. Jesus: The good man out of his good store gives good things; and the evil man out of his evil store gives evil things. Matthew 12:35.

Reality always shows up in the end, even if it does not always happen in the present. The mind often creates an identity that should suit the role you want to play. Behind a pious smile can be evil thoughts and intentions. This darkness and evil will sooner or later appear. Evil exists because of ignorance. If you are unable to predict the consequences of your actions, you are not capable of realizing that wrong actions lead to suffering both for the environment and for yourself. What is good and

*what is evil can vary depending on the level of aware-
ness you are acting from the outside. This can vary over
a life cycle. A person, who is established in Consciousness and has gained knowledge about life and existence,
always acts for the good of the whole and the good. He,
who is firm in the mind and ego, acts primarily for his
own good. The dysfunctional ego often acts without
thinking about the consequences of a certain action. An
action that usually takes place without compassion and
humility. Evil can be handled in different ways; meeting
evil with evil reinforces evil, meeting it with love can
in some cases reduce evil but in other situations evil
can be strengthened by feeling threatened. Approaching
evil with neutrality and distancing can mean that evil
remains latent and inactive. To relate, being consciously
present rooted in Consciousness, adapted to the prevailing situation, is the best approach, to evil.*

**If a person wants to be spiritually pure, what should
he start with?**

*42. Jesus: first make clean the inside of the cup and of
the plate, so that the outside may become equally clean.
Matthew 23:26.*

*Man has always been most focused on the external ap-
pearance. Maintaining inner purity should be at least as
important even more important. Giving the body fresh*

and healthy food and keeping it physically in good shape without drugs and toxins, provides a good basis for the body to stay healthy and thus the best condition for positive spiritual development. Both the body and the mental mind are tools that must be kept in good condition. Then positive energy is created. Inner purity is achieved by living life so that anxiety, stress and tension are not established. If impurities still exist, one can use prayer, some meditation technique or mental technique, which can help to provide a conscious presence in the Consciousness. Taking attention to the Consciousness contributes to an internal purification taking place completely automatically. This internal cleansing leads to the fact that you also want to keep the physical body clean and fresh. He who is pure inside radiates this purity both spiritually and physically.

You are called the Son of Man and King of the Jews, what is your mission and why are you here on earth?
43. Jesus: For truly the Son of man did not come to have servants, but to be a servant, and to give his life for the salvation of men. Mark 10:45.

The Son of Man, i.e. he who is established in Consciousness, does not need to be served as a king who is dependent on power, prestige and honor. Since the human son has no ego that needs to assert him, he can act as a tool to help his fellow human beings to become perfect and spiritually aware, i.e. to serve humanity.

How should I behave in meeting other people?
44. Jesus: Have love for your neighbour as for yourself. Mark 12:31.

You must love your neighbor as yourself, as you and your neighbor are one and the same based on Consciousness, i.e. there is only one Consciousness, one God one existence. When awareness identifies with Consciousness, there is no duality, only unity. When one is present at this level of consciousness, there are no conflicts and aggression but only compassion, humility, mercy and unconditional love. When one acts on the basis of this level of awareness of pure Consciousness, there is no other possibility than love. The conditions are then good for the identification with the mind and ego to disappear and then the presence in the Consciousness becomes conscious. This does not mean that the mind and ego disappear, they remain as tools to be able to navigate life, but they no longer form the basis of identity.

When someone gains spiritual insight, why is it difficult for him to be accepted by the closest circle of friends?

45. Jesus: No prophet is honored in his country. Luke 4:24.

As long as the mind rules over awareness, the mind makes relative judgments between itself and the environment. The mind judges and ranks on the basis of the experiences one has from the past. If someone who is judged to be an ordinary person pretends to be a "prophet", i.e. a spiritual person who is aware of Consciousness or Spirit, one becomes suspicious and has difficulty ignoring the particular perception one has previously created about that person. Jealousy can also occur, i.e. you ask yourself; why has that person achieved spiritual insight and not me.

If you have different opinions, conflict often arises, how to avoid conflicts?

46. Jesus: Be not judges of others, and you will not be judged. Luke 6:37.

The mind has a habit of also wanting to judge after an assessment. It is then often the ego that wants to stand out at the expense of the environment. If two egos with this attitude meet, a conflict often arises when both want to be right, assert themselves and judge. A conscious individual can accept life as it is without having to assert itself and has no need to judge life. This will then not be drawn into unnecessary strife and conflict. If you do not need to judge life, you will not be judged by life either. You also do not have to judge yourself when you have made a mistake, it is better to learn from the mistakes and move on with a focus on being aware in the present. Focusing on mistakes you have made in the past gives both negative energy in body and mind and means that you can lose contact with reality in the now.

How should one relate to greed and selfishness?

47. Jesus: Give, and it will be given to you. Luke 6:38.

This is a universal law, i.e. that what you give or send out you get back. Both the good and the bad that you give to life you get back from life. The ego often wants to blame the environment when something bad happens, when in fact it is a repercussion on something that the individual himself has done. Greed and selfishness i.e. the desire for power and to own is the greatest and fundamental problem of mankind. Many problems are rooted in greed; climate threats, war, poverty, dictatorships and corruption. Greed is dependent on the ego dominating consciousness. Only by letting go of the ego can one give instead of take. Greed is largely due to a lack of compassion and solidarity.

The more compassion there is in consciousness the less greed and vice versa, the more greed the less compassion. This applies to both individuals and societal structures.

How should one relate to power, honor and fame?
48. Jesus: For what profit will a man have if he gets the entire world, but undergoes loss or destruction himself? Luke 9:25.

Creating an identity through possessions, power and fame provides a temporary satisfaction for the ego. At the same time, this identity creates a shielding and distancing from the Self or Consciousness. Being present in Consciousness provides a permanent satisfaction that is not dependent on ownership, power and fame. It is not the property, the power or the fame that is the problem but the relationship to them. The richest man in the world could be established in Consciousness and completely free from attachments to the worldly, while a poor man who only owns the clothes on the body and a begging bowl could be totally bound by these possessions and completely unable to direct attention inward to Consciousness . It is thus not the worldly that is the problem, but the relationship to the worldly, i.e. since all attention and awareness is established on the worldly, there is no contact with the inner Consciousness. Only he who can be unbound in relation to the world can still be present without losing Himself.

How should one relate to the desire for material possessions?

49. Jesus: Take care to keep yourselves free from the desire for property; for a man's life is not made up of the number of things which he has. Luke 12:15.

One reason why one does not want to focus attention inward and surrender to Consciousness, is the desire for power, honor, and possessions. As long as this desire governs a person's awareness, he is stuck in worldly existence. When one finally realizes that the worldly does not give any permanent joy and satisfaction, the worldly desire to have can be transformed into a spiritual desire, i.e. one becomes a seeker of inner self-sufficiency and union with the true identity. Only when this is a fact can real happiness, peace and satisfaction prevail and one realizes that the desire for power, honor and possessions was only a surrogate.

How should one relate to the urge to drink alcohol when life feels worrying?

50. Jesus: But give attention to yourselves, for fear that your hearts become over-full of the pleasures of food and wine, and the cares of this life, and that day may come on you suddenly, and take you as in a net. Luke 21:34.

The mind wants attention and satisfaction in order to exist. Therefore, the mind constantly wants to be occupied with satisfying needs of various kinds e.g. to shop for goods or to eat and drink. The ego and the intellect create individual desires and needs that must be satisfied in the future. Being influenced by alcohol or drugs keeps the awareness in the mind. Often alcohol stimulates the dysfunctional dark side of the ego. The intoxication, which from the beginning in a smaller amount can be perceived as uplifting and positive, becomes the opposite with a larger amount, i.e. evokes aggression and indiscretion when the dark side of the ego emerges. Alcohol and drugs break down the body's natural response mechanisms and you become more susceptible to various diseases.

If I drink in my loneliness, no one knows anything about it.

51. Jesus: God sees your hearts. Luke 16:15.

God is omnipresent, i.e. present in everything, everywhere and has control from the smallest particle to the whole mental so-called physical universe. God's Consciousness encompasses everything and all levels of awareness in all organic life. So there is no thought or expression of emotion that goes unnoticed. God knows all the lies and everything that one tries to hide. So you do not have to inform God about the problems and needs you have in prayer. God is everything and knows everything. The Kingdom of God is what is.

Is it easier to enter the kingdom of God if you are rich?

52. Jesus: It is simpler for a camel to go through the eye of a needle, than for a man who has much money to come into the kingdom of God. Luke 18:25.

The desire for wealth and power means that attention is drawn to external existence. When one is firmly rooted in the mind, the driving force is the desire for pleasure, wealth, power and position. The goal of attention becomes the aspects of the mind that provide the most satisfaction and security for the moment. It becomes a constant pursuit of sensual satisfaction. This means the desire to enter the kingdom of God, i.e. to the inner existence comes second and then becomes in principle an impossibility. It is not the wealth itself that is the problem, but the constant desire for wealth. As the desire for wealth is prioritized, the kingdom of God will not be experienced.

What is it that gives real satisfaction in this life? What is the water of life?

53. Jesus: Everyone who takes this water will be in need

*of it again: But whoever takes the water I give him will
never be in need of drink again; for the water I give him
will become in him a fountain of eternal life. John 4:14.
The desires that one has for worldly position and power
as well as for material possessions are never definitively
satisfied. The mind constantly requires new experiences
and stimuli. Material life becomes a constant pursuit of
satisfaction that will never become permanent. Turning
attention inward means that the influence of Consciousness provides a constant flow of self-sufficiency. One
does not then have to strive for satisfaction as this state
gives incessant inner satisfaction regardless of external
events and objects.*

**What should I work for and pay attention to, so that
my existence here on earth will be of the greatest
benefit?**

*54. Jesus: Let your work not be for the food which comes
to an end, but for the food which goes on for eternal life.
John 6:27.*

*Being constantly engaged in external activities gives a
drain of energy while attention to the inner, to Consciousness, gives a constant flow of energy. To have a
constant presence in eternity and at the same time be
engaged in the perishable world is the ultimate presence
in the total existence. It then becomes food that provides*

the greatest nourishment and energy for both the worldly and the spiritual existence. Jesus expresses the danger of being one-sidedly focused on the transient, i.e. which is born, maintained and dies. The transient must be put in relation to that which is eternal and without change, that which has always existed and will always exist without undergoing any change, i.e. an absolute Being.

What is it that gets eternal life; the body dies after a number of years?
55. Jesus: The spirit is the life giver; the flesh is of no value: the words which I have said to you are spirit and they are life. John 6:63.

The spirit is life, the life force; there is only one spirit a Consciousness and a life, while the "flesh" i.e. the body is individual as it belongs to the relatively changing material existence. The body is born, maintained and dies, it is only a temporary tool for the eternal Spirit.

Where do speech and thoughts come from and how does one who is aware of the Father speak?
56. Jesus: The man whose words come from himself is looking for glory for himself, but he who is looking for the glory of him who sent him that man is true and there is no evil in him. John 7:18.

Speech and thoughts can either come from the individual intellect or directly from Godconsciousness. The speech of the individual intellect is often colored by selfish purposes such as honor and exercise of power. When speech is rooted in Godconsciousness, a speech arises based on wisdom and truth. This speech has no other purpose than to express the truth. There are then no personal purposes but only a need to express the intuitive feeling that exists beyond the intellect. Personal memories and experiences can of course be helpful when navigating one's way in life, but they can also preserve a certain point of view so that new insights cannot emerge. Jesus who spoke from Consciousness became a representative of this state of awareness in the relative existence.

How can man become free?

57. Jesus: And you will have knowledge of what is true, and that will make you free. John 8:32.

Finding one's true identity is truth and true freedom. As long as one identifies with the mind, ego and body, one is bound by duality, i.e. the relatively changing existence and thus with a temporary surrogate identity. As time goes on, the mind gains new experiences and acquires new identities that affect the mind and also the body ages and changes. Consciousness is independent of the passage of time and the external world. When one is present in Consciousness one is totally independent of worldly judgments and illusions. This is the only true freedom and the ultimate truth.

What will be the consequences of deliberately acting in the wrong way, i.e. to sin?
58. Jesus: Truly I say to you! Everyone who does evil is the servant of sin. John 8:34.

What is sin? It is to deliberately act in a wrong way that has negative effects on the environment and ultimately on oneself. Ultimately, such action is due to unconsciousness towards life as a whole and this deficiency is in turn due to not having contact with life and Consciousness. The negative effects that sin entails bind man to the actions and its effects; one becomes a slave to sin. This contributes to the fact that one finds it difficult to free oneself from the mind and ego and becomes unable to pay attention to Consciousness. In order for this not to become a negative spiral, one must consciously act so that awareness of Consciousness arises. By turning attention inward through prayer, meditation, or through other spiritual or therapeutic methods, one can find oneself. This requires a commitment and a willingness to leave the negative unconscious existence. When the suffering has become great enough, you may have to change and start looking for better alternatives. Suffering is thus an alarm clock that awakens to a higher awareness. Suffering in itself is not good but it acts as a guide to self-awareness and awareness of Consciousness. Suffering can thus function as a necessary evil that leads to something good. Sin and suffering are intimately linked as they form the basis of the relationship between cause and effect or "what you sow you may also reap".

What are the consequences of actions that I perform, but that I am not aware that they are wrong?
59. Whatever seed a man puts in, that will he get back as grain. The Book of Galatians 6:7.

Actions in the present have consequences in the future and they may be due to causes from the past, is logical, i.e. that there is a cause and an effect. This law is found in most religions, such as Christianity. In Buddhism and Hinduism it is called the law of karma. The law of karma exists only in the relative existence to provide experiences that will lead to awareness and hopefully lead to a state of presence that enables Godconsciousness to become conscious. Once this awareness is established, the law of karma has fulfilled its function. The mind is bound to the law of cause and effect. Everything that the mind does has a repercussion that affects the individual. "What you sow, you also reap." This means that the mind is dependent on acting in time and space. Without the past and the future, the law of cause and effect could not exist. The nature of the mind is to relate to the past and to the future, it is a prerequisite for the mind to be able to function. Through the law of cause and effect, the individual himself creates his dualistic, relative existence in time and space.

What is the difference between a spiritually conscious person and a person living in ignorance of the spiritual reality?

60. Jesus: A man may go about in the day without falling, because he sees the light of this world. But if a man goes about in the night, he may have a fall because the light is not in him. John. 11: 9-10.

He who is aware of Consciousness observes the world and is not bound by it. Living then becomes a life without resistance and problems. This gives a bright view of life. If you are bound to the mind, you become dependent on the world and its problems and suffering. You are then in a state of consciousness that often gives a dark view of life.

How should one relate to the spiritual light?

61. Jesus: In so far as you have the light put your faith in the light so that you may become sons of light. John 12:36.

When one is established in Consciousness, an inner light often arises that does not come from any artificial light source. It can be experienced as if the inner existence is filled with light and that it is an ease to live and move in the outer existence. People who are rooted in this level of awareness are often called enlightened, what is also characteristic is that they are present in a real identity and not in the false ego identity of the mind. The enlightened are the sons and daughters of light. Everyone is on the way to the light, even if it is not established under the current life situation.

How does the spiritual light affect?

62. Jesus: There is light within a person of light, and it shines on the whole world. If it does not shine, it is dark. Thomas 24.

The enlightened become like lighthouses in darkness, they light up so that others can also become aware of the light. The collective state of consciousness of the earth is very strongly influenced by every enlightened master. The more people who reach this state of Consciousness, the easier it will be to establish it for others. In the end, both the individual and the collective consciousness are enlightened. The stronger the light, the weaker the darkness.

Is there a path that leads to the Father?

63. Jesus: I am the true and living way: no one comes to the Father but by me. If you had knowledge of me, you would have knowledge of my Father. John 14:6-7.

Jesus was established in the Kingdom of Heaven. When he said "The kingdom of heaven is within you", this was not a belief or speculation; it was an established level of consciousness. He knew from experience that the Father is within us. When he had attained this state of consciousness he could claim that he had found the way to the Kingdom of Heaven, this state of consciousness which is the highest truth of life. Establishing this state of consciousness is not an intellectual process or belief, it is a reality and a development of awareness that everyone can undergo just as Jesus had done. This is the most primary thing in life, everything else is secondary. God, Heaven, Consciousness and Life are one and the same. The Consciousness that Jesus refers to when he says that he is; the way, the truth and the life are not a belief but based on a real self-perceived reality. He has chosen a path that has given him the truth, a truth that is based on real life. This truth is not based on a belief or philosophy about life. He was so established in the Father i.e. The Kingdom of Heaven that he could claim that if you knew him, you would automatically know the Kingdom of Heaven. This state of consciousness becomes a reality when one has the courage and is ready to let go of the sensual and selfish identity and be completely present in the real spiritual identity. The divine identity is not limited by time and space, it is eternal and present without any limitation. This state of Consciousness is not dependent on the intellect but generates wisdom through intuition.

What is the most important thing to get to know during mortality?

64. Jesus: Those who know all, but are lacking in themselves, are utterly lacking. Thomas 67.

Being a book scholar and having knowledge of the external existence does not have to mean that you have knowledge of the internal existence. Knowledge comes from outside via e.g. teachers or books while wisdom comes from within as clarity or clairvoyance without the intervention of the intellect. It may be that if you are a professor with a great deal of knowledge in a field of knowledge, you identify yourself with the title professor, but this only means that in a certain limited field of knowledge you have documented more knowledge about the relative existence than most people. This does not mean that you automatically gain access to wisdom and can identify with who you are. You can still lack the most important knowledge, i.e. the ability to observe the mind, body and external existence from Consciousness. Only when one can identify with the true spiritual Self with the observer, i.e. The Kingdom of Heaven or Consciousness, the primary knowledge has been established. Trying to get to know oneself (his Self i.e. Consciousness) from the intellect and the mind is doomed to fail. It only gives confusion and uncertainty about who you think you are. One will never find the true identity through the intellect and the mind, only false identities, but one can learn the functioning of the mind and how the mind communicates with the environment.

Who are you?

65. Jesus: I am the light that is over all things. I am all: from me all came forth, and to me all attained. Thomas 77.

When one is present in Consciousness, knowledge of existence automatically arises. Then you can say that "Consciousness is everything" and "Everything has started from Consciousness" it is not a belief or speculation but concrete experiences based on Consciousness. It is God, i.e. Consciousness that has created everything and is constantly creating in the present in the relative external existence. Consciousness is the creator, the created and has the creative ability and is consciously present throughout creation. When Jesus says that he is All, this is not speculation or faith but a real state of real consciousness in which Jesus lives. When Jesus says; "from me all came forth and to me all attained" he refers to the process of creation, i.e. the physical material process of creation that is manifested from the Consciousness.

Is the one who finds himself also recognized by the world?

66. Jesus: Those who have found themselves, of them the world is not worthy. Thomas 111.

He who is established and present in Consciousness cannot be judged by the world, i.e. the prevailing level of collective awareness, as there is no knowledge and no spiritual references to be able to make a correct assessment. The world judges on the basis of the prevailing collective level of consciousness which so far has incomplete knowledge of Consciousness and the identification with it and presence in it.

What happens if you receive spiritual guidance from someone who is not established in the truth?

67. Jesus: "If a blind person leads a blind person, both of them will fall into a hole." Thomas 34.

There is a risk in trusting someone who pretends to have the truth, but who is not present in Consciousness

*and thus does not have access to true spiritual knowl-
edge. The guiding person is also at risk of experiencing
setbacks that affect him or her negatively. The person is
especially negatively affected if he is looking for power,
honor and wealth.*

How should one relate to those who act incorrectly out of ignorance?

*68. Jesus: Father, let them have forgiveness, for they have
no knowledge of what they are doing. Luke 23:34.*

*Since you are not aware of what you are doing, you
should not be punished but forgiven. Sometimes you
have to be able to let mercy go before justice. Jesus was
conscious, but saw that his fellow human beings were
not. He identified with the Father and from this level of
consciousness there is no judgment but only forgiveness.
If he had identified with the mind and the ego, he would
have automatically wanted to judge and punish his fellow human beings when they crucified him and shared
his clothes among themselves. Forgiveness means that
conflicts and enmity can be avoided. After forgiveness,
both parties can move on with peace of mind and thus
they have avoided conflicts and enmity being stored in
the future.*

Is there any purpose to human suffering?

69. Jesus: Congratulations to the person who has suffered and has found life. Thomas 58.

Suffering in itself is not worth striving for. However, suffering fulfills an important function for man to be able to experience states of awareness that lead to suffering and states that bring happiness and spiritual satisfaction. It can be said that suffering is a necessary evil and painful, but at the same time a guide to something good and to a brighter existence. But it requires that man be sensitive and prone to change in order not to get caught up in suffering. No one escapes suffering; it nurtures and develops awareness to result in the pure love that is the fundamental tone of the universe. The suffering often occurs due to ignorance. Wanting to do evil deeds that lead to suffering is often dependent on ignorance. The ego believes it can gain benefits by asserting itself in various ways at the expense of the environment, even if it results in the environment suffering. The ego does not always expect that a certain action will have consequences and that the effect of the action will always ultimately affect the individual himself. This is the hard school of life. If you can´t mentally distinguish between good and evil, you must concretely experience the difference. That is why nothing happens by chance. You can always harvest what you have sown yourself.

*We are always responsible for what we are doing and
what life gives us, whether it is suffering, happiness or
peace. Suffering is a contrast to happiness and harmony.
In the relative existence, opposite contexts must always
exist, such as that light cannot exist without darkness.
Suffering is not always created by some conscious evil
but sometimes also by an unconscious ignorance of
existence. Suffering is a reaction to this ignorance and
the behavior that ignorance is the cause of. As long as
there is a cause for suffering, suffering will be the result.
Historically, humanity has always been trapped in
suffering. Suffering has been considered as something
inevitable that belongs to life and man has not even
tried to free himself from suffering. It has even become
the case that suffering has been glorified by writers,
poets, musicians, artists and media creators. They have
been recognized and praised for their ability to portray
suffering. The media has created a need to consume
suffering. Suffering has in some cases become a way to
achieve sensory satisfaction. You are affected by both
collective and individual suffering. Suffering affects both
the body and the mind. Consciousness is not affected
as suffering is only related to the relative aspect of life.
Since existence cannot be separated from cause and
effect, suffering is a constant reality on the relative
plane. The mind participates in suffering. It is not an
intellectual attitude that determines the relationship to*

suffering, but the prevailing state of awareness. Suffering itself does not give rise to any bondage, just as the pursuit of happiness itself is not the cause of bondage. It is the prevailing state of consciousness that determines whether attachment to suffering and happiness or inner peace should arise. If you experience more suffering than you can experience, you become unconscious, i.e. consciousness is turned off and one loses contact with the body and mind. Not being able to accept life as it is, always leads to conflict and suffering. When awareness is present in Consciousness, it is possible to accept life in step one and in step two try to influence life if one is dissatisfied with the present and if it is not possible to influence the present, in step three plan to influence in the future, thus avoiding dissatisfaction, conflict and suffering. If it is not possible to influence an event, you must accept it. This can be difficult for the mind if the event does not match the ego's desires. To be present in the Consciousness and to have complete confidence in it is to leave the mental suffering. Of course, the body can still cause suffering, especially when it gets old and worn out. It is not uncommon for someone who is dying and experiencing extreme suffering, to suddenly experience that the suffering begins to subside and that silence, light and peace appear. What has happened then is that awareness has been drawn to Consciousness and the mind and body have been transcended, a new state of consciousness has been established. Awareness then begins to leave body and mind and the so-called death approaches.

Where is your home?

70. Jesus: The foxes have holes and the birds of heaven have a resting-place, but the Son of Man has nowhere to put his head. Matthew 8:20.

The Son of Man is not bound to any physical place that's normally called his home. The home is the state of Consciousness. The Son of Man rests in the Consciousness of God while being present in the physical relative existence. This state of Consciousness means perfection.

How does creation work?

(The following verse contains answers from the Gospel of John in the Bible, not from Jesus).

71. From the first he was the Word and the Word was in relation with God and was God. This Word was from the first in relation with God. All things came into existence through him, and without him nothing was. What came into existence in him was life, and the life was the light of men. John 1: 1-4. In the relative time dimension of existence, time is a concept, i.e. the past, the present and the future. These time concepts are created by man to put the relative existence on an imaginary time axis that begins with the beginning or a creation. In the relative existence there is always a beginning and an end. The absolute eternal aspect of existence is not a man-made concept, but the eternal state of being. The word that in the Bible quote symbolizes God's eternal ability to create is a link between the relatively change-able and the absolute eternal being. Through the word is manifested a sound and a thought that becomes a relative creation in the relative existence. This creation always takes place in the eternal present. God's eternal life permeates the entire relatively changing creation and both life i.e. Consciousness and light are links between the absolute eternal and the relatively changing cre-ation. Consciousness is always present in the now both in organic life and inorganic matter as energy. Consciousness is present as the observer of organic life and has complete control over the inorganic matter from the smallest particle to the largest universe.

What is God's name?

72. And Moses said to God, When I come to the children of Israel and say to them, the God of your fathers has sent me to you: and they say to me, what is his name? What am I to say to them? And God said to him, I AM WHAT I AM: and he said, Say to the children of Israel, I AM has sent me to you. Exodus 3:13-14.

God can not be described in words. There are no words or concepts that can fully describe the absolute eternal Consciousness of God, as it is not as the relatively changing aspect of God of existence is limited to time and space. To say "I am" refers to that which is not changeable and transient but that which is eternal, indestructible, without beginning and without end.

To say; I am a man or I am old, means that you make a conceptual description that the intellect uses. It is not possible to describe God with intellectual concepts. Therefore, the closest you can come is to say "I am", when you have to express God or Consciousness. God says to Moses "I am" to avoid all unnecessary concepts and descriptions, as there is nothing relative, perishable to be described.

Consciousness is eternally present everywhere regardless of time and space, i.e. there is nowhere or in something where it is not present. It is the cause of the manifestation of the relative material changing existence. Consciousness does not change, no experience is gained and no awareness disappears. This level of consciousness is eternal and unaffected by relative time. Absolute Consciousness is the basis of relative existence and both parts are interdependent in order for existence to exist. One can say that the absolute is nothing manifested (no things) while the relative is everything manifested (all things). They are opposites of each other but at the same time they cannot exist separately.

When there is awareness in Consciousness, one can only describe it as "I am". Consciousness is neither conceptual nor descriptive. "I am" cannot be an opposite of anything, as it is all existence and presence. There is no dualistic relationship to "I am" or Consciousness, which is the only true identity. To be present in Consciousness is non-dualism, i.e. unity-consciousness , which means being one with the total existence.

As awareness is present in Consciousness, this generates a state that is without activity. When awareness is inactive, it can be in stillness and in inner peace. To be simultaneously aware of the relative changing existence means to be completely in unity with what is, i.e. the totality of Consciousness which means undivided, simultaneous presence in both the relative and the absolute existence. Silence, stillness and emptiness then also go hand in hand with activity, presence of mind and fullness, perfection is then a reality. Reality and Truth are then established.

Is there anything else important that is written in the Holy Scriptures?

73. In quiet and rest is your salvation: peace and hope are your strength. Jesaja 30:15.

Silence i.e. non-activity is the basis of activity. Being united with Consciousness automatically provides stillness as well as presence and confidence in the present. If the mind wants to create this state by trying to stop the thought process, only a conflict arises that leads to tension instead of relaxation. It is not possible to become aware of Consciousness through the mind. Therefore, one can give up all attempts to, through the intellect and the logical thinking, become aware of Consciousness. The entrance ticket is instead to, without conflict with the mind, by accepting the mind as it is, be able to leave the mind and be completely effortless and present in Consciousness. This is not an intellectual process but a state of spontaneous abandonment of the mind, ego and intellect as a reference and thus total awareness is obtained. Saints, mystics and spiritual preachers have always spoken of prayer and meditation as an aid to achieving silence. Thereby an opportunity arises to release the activity of the mind and experience Consciousness which results in absolute silence.

74. Amen! Revelation 3:14

Jesus calls himself "he who is Amen" which means the credible and truthful witness. To witnessing existence means that one is not bound by the mind and the relatively manifested existence but established on the eternal, unmanifest level of Consciousness where one is aware in Consciousness. Based on this level of Consciousness, one is a credible and true witness of the relative existence. Existence is observed without judging or being bound by it.

Amen also has the meaning "let your will be done", i.e. to surrender to Consciousness.

The word "Amen" can be used to pay attention to in prayer and in meditation. By following Jesus' instruction to "enter into your chamber and pray to the Father in secret, then you will have power when the Holy Spirit (the helper) comes upon you and helps you with the whole truth, you will be perfected and become one ". Being aware in Consciousness means that the dualistic relationship of faith has become a non-dualistic relationship, bringing the realization that you are Consciousness. At the absolute eternal level there is only one state of Consciousness, at the relative changeable level there are many different states of awareness, where the degree of consciousness varies.

(The quotes from 'Thomasevangeliet' are gathered from the website"Allt om Bibeln". HYPERLINK "http://www. alltombibeln.se/"www.alltombibeln.se)

Index

Bible quotes with reference to verses in the Bible or the Gospel of Thomas;

1. Jesus: The kingdom of God will not come through observation, and men will not say, see, it is here! Or, there! For the kingdom of God is within you. Luke 17: 20-21.
2. Jesus: But when you make your prayer, go into your private room, and, shutting the door, say a prayer to your Father in secret, and your Father, who sees in secret, will give you your reward. Matthew 6:7.
3. Jesus: And I say to you, make requests, and they will be answered; what you are searching for, you will get; when you give the sign, the door will be open to you. Luke 11:9.
4. Jesus: Make no store of wealth for yourselves on earth, where it may be turned to dust by worms and weather, and where thieves may come in by force and take it away. But make a store for yourselves in heaven, where it will not be turned to dust and where thieves do not come in to take it away, for where your wealth is, there will your heart be. Matthew 6:19-21.
5. Jesus: But let your first care be for his kingdom and

*his righteousness; and all these other things will be given
to you in addition. Matthew 6:33.*

*6. Jesus: He who has the desire to keep his life will have
it taken from him, and he who gives up his life because
of me will have it given back to him. Matthew 10:39.*

*7. Jesus: Truly, I say to you, If you do not have a change
of heart and become like little children, you will not go
into the kingdom of heaven. Whoever, then, will make
himself as low as this little child, the same is the greatest
in the kingdom of heaven. Matthew 18:3-4.*

*8. Jesus: Truly I say to you, whatever things are fixed
by you on earth will be fixed in heaven: and whatever
you make free on earth will be made free in heaven.
Matthew 18:18.*

*9. Jesus: So the last will be first and the first last. But
if anyone has a desire to become great among you, let
him be your servant and whoever has a desire to be first
among you, let him take the lowest place. Even as the
Son of man did not come to have servants, but to be
a servant, and to give his life for the salvation of men.
Matthew 20: 16, 20:26.*

*10. Jesus continued: For every man who gives himself
a high place will be put down, but he who takes a low
place will be lifted up. Luke 14:11.*

*11. Jesus: If any man has the desire to come after me, let
him give up all other desires, and take up his cross and
come after me. Mark 8:34.*

12. Jesus: My kingdom is not of this world. John 18:36.

13. Jesus: You are to keep watch: because you are not certain when the master of the house is coming ! Mark 13:35.

 14. Jesus: Truly, I say to you, without a new birth no man is able to see the kingdom of God. John 3:3.

15. Jesus: Truly, I say to you, If a man's birth is not from water and from the Spirit, it is not possible for him to go into the kingdom of God. That which has birth from the flesh is flesh, and that which has birth from the Spirit is spirit. John 3:5-6.

16. Jesus: I am the door: if any man goes in through me he will have salvation John 10:9.

17. Jesus: I and my Father are one. The Father is in me and I am in the Father. John 10:30 and 38.

18. Jesus: when he, the Spirit of true knowledge, has come, he will be your guide into all true knowledge. John 16:13.

19. Jesus: Holy Father, keep them in your name which you have given to me, so that they may be one even as we are one. John 17;11
and;
The glory which you hav e given to me I have given to them, so that they may be one even as we are one. Joh 17:22.

20. Jesus: You will have power, when the Holy Spirit has come on you . The acts. 1:8.

21. Jesus: The Helper, the Holy Spirit, whom the Father will send in my name, will be your teacher in all things and will put you in mind of everything I have said to you. May peace be with you; my peace I give to you. John 14:26-27.

22. Jesus: The Father's imperial rule is inside you and outside you. When you know yourselves, then you will be known, and you will understand that you are children of the living Father. But if you do not know yourselves, then you live in poverty, and you are the poverty. Thomas 3.

23. Jesus: When you make the two into one, and when you make the inner like the outer and the outer like the inner, and the upper like the lower, and when you make male and female into a single one, so that the male will not be male nor the female be female Thomas 22.

24. Jesus: What is the evidence of your Father in you? It is motion and rest. Thomas 50.

25. Jesus: If one is whole, one will be filled with light, but if one is divided, one will be filled with darkness. Thomas 61.

26. Jesus: If you do not fast from the world, you will not find the Father's domain. Thomas 27.

27. Jesus: The Father's imperial rule is spread out upon the earth, and people don't see it. Thomas 113.

28. If any man has a desire to come after me, let him give up all, and take up his cross every day, and come after me. Luke 9:23.

29 Jesus: Then have no care for tomorrow: tomorrow will take care of itself. Take the trouble of the day as it comes. Matthew 6:34.

30. Jesus: No man, having put his hand to the plough and looking back, is good enough for the kingdom of God. Luke. 9:62.

31. Jesus: For this reason I say to you, take no thought for your life, about what food you will take, or for your body, how it may be clothed. Is not life more than food, and the body than its clothing? Give thought to the ravens; they do not put seeds into the earth, or get together grain; they have no store-houses or buildings; and God gives them their food: of how much greater value are you than the birds! But let your chief care be for his kingdom, and these other things will be given to you in addition. Luk.12:22-23, 31..

32. Jesus fortsatte: Don't fret, from morning to evening and from evening to morning, about what you're going to wear. Thomas 36.

33. Jesus: He who is in love with life will have it taken from him; and he who has no care for his life in this world will keep it for ever and ever. John 12:25.

34. Jesus: Do not make use of force against an evil man; but to him who gives you a blow on the right side of your face let the left be turned. Matthew 5:39.

35. Jesus: Put up your sword again into its place: for all those who take the sword will come to death by the sword. Matthew 26:52.

36. *Jesus: but I say to you, have love for those who are against you, and make prayer for those who are cruel to you Matthew 5:44.*

37. *Jesus: why do you take note of the grain of dust in your brother's eye, but take no note of the bit of wood which is in your eye? Matthew 7:3.*

38. *Jesus: Do not give that which is holy to the dogs, or put your jewels before pigs, for fear that they will be crushed under foot by the pigs whose attack will then be made against you. Matthew 7:6.*

39. *Jesus: Give to Caesar the things which are Caesar's, and to God the things which are God's. Matthew 22:21.*

40. *Jesus: All those things, then, which you would have men do to you, even so do you to them. Matthew 7:12.*

41. *Jesus: The good man out of his good store gives good things; and the evil man out of his evil store gives evil things. Matthew 12:35.*

42. *Jesus: For truly the Son of man did not come to have servants, but to be a servant, and to give his life for the salvation of men. Mark 10:45.*

43. *Jesus: first make clean the inside of the cup and of the plate, so that the outside may become equally clean. Matthew 23:26.*

44. *Jesus: Have love for your neighbour as for yourself. Mark 12:31.*

45. *Jesus: No prophet is honored in his country. Luke 4:24.*

46. Jesus: Be not judges of others, and you will not be judged. Luke 6:37.

47. Jesus: Give, and it will be given to you. Luke 6:38.

48. Jesus: For what profit will a man have if he gets all the world, but undergoes loss or destruction himself? Luke 9:25.

49. Jesus: Take care to keep yourselves free from the desire for property; for a man's life is not made up of the number of things which he has. Luke 12:15.

50. Jesus: But give attention to yourselves, for fear that your hearts become over-full of the pleasures of food and wine, and the cares of this life, and that day may come on you suddenly, and take you as in a net. Luke 21:34.

51. Jesus: God sees your hearts. Luke 16:15.

52. Jesus: It is simpler for a camel to go through the eye of a needle, than for a man who has much money to come into the kingdom of God. Luke 18:25.

53, Jesus: Everyone who takes this water will be in need of it again: But whoever takes the water I give him will never be in need of drink again; for the water I give him will become in him a fountain of eternal life. John 4:14.

54. Jesus: Let your work not be for the food which comes to an end, but for the food which goes on for eternal life. John 6:27.7

55. Jesus: The spirit is the life giver; the flesh is of no value: the words which I have said to you are spirit and they are life. John 6:63.

56. Jesus: The man whose words come from himself is looking for glory for himself, but he who is looking for the glory of him who sent him that man is true and there is no evil in him. John 7:18.

57. Jesus: And you will have knowledge of what is true, and that will make you free. John 8:32.

58. Jesus: Truly I say to you, Everyone who does evil is the servant of sin. John 8:34.

59. Whatever seed a man puts in, that will he get back as grain. The Book of Galatians 6:7.

60. Jesus: A man may go about in the day without falling, because he sees the light of this world. But if a man goes about in the night, he may have a fall because the light is not in him. John 11: 9-10.

61. Jesus: In so far as you have the light, put your faith in the light so that you may become sons of light. John 12:36.

62. Jesus: There is light within a person of light, and it shines on the whole world. If it does not shine, it is dark. Thomas 24.

63. Jesus: I am the true and living way: no one comes to the Father but by me. If you had knowledge of me, you would have knowledge of my Father. John 14:6-7.

64. Jesus: Those who know all, but are lacking in themselves, are utterly lacking. Thomas 67.

65. Jesus: I am the light that is over all things. I am all: from me all came forth, and to me all attained. Thomas 77.

66. Jesus: Those who have found themselves, of them the world is not worthy. Thomas 111.

67. Jesus: "If a blind person leads a blind person, both of them will fall into a hole." Thomas 34.

68. Jesus: Father, let them have forgiveness, for they have no knowledge of what they are doing. Luke 23:34.

69 Jesus: Congratulations to the person who has toiled and has found life. Thomas 58.

70. Jesus: The foxes have holes and the birds of heaven have a resting-place, but the Son of Man has nowhere to put his head. Matthew 8:20.

71. From the first he was the Word, and the Word was in relation with God and was God. This Word was from the first in relation with God. All things came into existence through him, and without him nothing was. What came into existence in him was life, and the life was the light of men. John 1: 1-4.

72. And Moses said to God, When I come to the children of Israel and say to them, The God of your fathers has sent me to you: and they say to me, What is his name? what am I to say to them? And God said to him, I AM WHAT I AM: and he said, Say to the children of Israel, I AM has sent me to you. Exodus 3:13-14.

73. In quiet and rest is your salvation: peace and hope are your strength Jesaja 30:15.

74. Amen! Revelation 3:14